MAUDE

Minneapolis

FIRST EDITION April 2026

10 9 8 7 6 5 4 3 2 1

ISBN: 978-1-962834-73-5
Cover and interior design by Gary Lindberg
Historical Images of Dinkytown and the West Bank used with permission from Hennepin County Library Special Collections

Maude

Helen Electrie Lindsay

Minneapolis

Also by Helen Electrie Lindsay

Written on the Knee:
A Diary from the Greek-Italian Front of WWII

PROLOGUE

It's February of 2003 and Judy, Andy, Hugh and I sit around the dining room table celebrating Judy's birthday and reminiscing about the old days.

Al's Breakfast, 1974

We've all known each other for over thirty-five years. Back in the late '60s we hung around the East and

West Bank of the Mississippi at the University of Minnesota. Dinkytown was the hub of our universe. Late night parties that started at the Mixer's on the West Bank and ended up at Judy's apartment. Early morning omelets at Al's and Sunday lunches at Mama D's.

Mixer's Bar on the West Bank, 1974

Hughie pours some wine and softly asks, "What's your music preference?"

"Anything, as long as it is not the news..." I quickly reply and then add, "I really don't want to hear any more about the invasion of Iraq…"

"Did you guys hear that between six and ten million people in at least 800 cities protested the war?" Andy fills in.

"Please, let's have music. But no protest songs. Maybe a waltz or even a polka for my birthday," Judy says.

"What happened, girl? Have you forgotten all the

anti-war demonstrations in Dinkytown back in '67-68? You lived in the heart of it," Andy asks.

"Yes, I remember. I still remember the people with signs that said, 'War is darkness, Peace is light' passing outside my window. But I don't want to hear it on my birthday!" Judy insisted.

"Remember when over 3,000 protesters blocked Washington Avenue in '72? … And the year Martin Luther King spoke against the war on campus and…oh yes, Eugene McCarthy and John Kerry spoke about 'dumping the war'… I think it was in some stadium. I suppose you'll say that they were all just Democrats." I said in one breath, trying not to give Judy a chance to think.

Judy immediately protested, "Why do you have to bring up politics? I thought we had a pact not to."

"Ok, politics, shmolitics… it's your birthday … I won't press it …" I said and quickly came up with a different memory to share.

"Say Judy, do you remember Mama D's restaurant and all the good times there?" I asked.

"Oh boy! Yes, I do. How do you remember all of that? You haven't lived on campus since 1969!" Judy exclaimed.

"What about the nomads, the beatniks, the counter-culture hippie bohemians who seamlessly moved from Dinkytown to East Hennepin, to Seven Corners to other places in the US 'from California to the New York Island'?" I asked, trying to stay off politics.

Judy quickly added, "Yes! Bob Dylan, Diamond Dave Whitaker, and Shadow?"

"Oh, *the* Diamond Dave? And Shadow! We never knew Shadow's real name… maybe he was Marv Davidov in disguise?" I said, laughing.

"Oh my God! Marv Davidson, the eternal non-violent protester, and Shadow! How could I forget Shadow? Everywhere we went he was always there, name unknown, identity unknown…" Judy blurted.

"Not Davidson, Davidov and his Honeywell project to oppose weapons made by them? He was the scourge of anyone with power, politicians, rich people, generals…" I chimed in. "What about Father Barry at the Newman Center who encouraged Catholics to become conscientious objectors? Besides, the Vietnam War protesters who hung around Dinkytown were revolutionary pioneers. Remember how they tried to stop them tearing down all those small businesses to build a stupid Red Barn? If the Dinkytown uprising had succeeded poor Dinkytown wouldn't have been junked…"

"I can't believe you remember all those crazies! The one I remember the most up to now is Shadow. All of that was so long ago and where have all those people gone?" Judy remarked.

"I don't know, but here we are still with war and darkness," I said.

"Please God, please! No more darkness, no more war, no killing anywhere in the world! We've had enough!" Judy replied

"She's right. Let's hope there will be no more darkness, no war and, pardon me, that 'Shrub' Bush won't invade Iraq," I said emphatically.

"I posted a picture of Bush looking like an ape at the bulletin board at work. All this talk about weapons of mass destruction is a lie. And they dragged poor Colin Powell into it with their conspiracy theories. His life and career will be destroyed forever," Hughie said in one breath.

"Bush as an ape? Why degrade a poor monkey like that?" Andy added with a smirk.

Then there was silence. I got up and went to the kitchen to check on the food. Then, like a wave of sea water splashing on the shore, memories filled my mind.

Judy, Andy, Hugh and I had all met before attending the University of Minnesota. After graduating, we magically reconnected in Dinkytown cafes and bars. I was finishing my degree in Physics, Hugh was finishing his law degree, Andy was in the Marines and was getting ready to be shipped to Vietnam, and Judy had gotten her first job as a teacher.

Back in the late '60s and early '70s Dinkytown and the West Bank were blossoming with ideas and visions that would transform American culture and society. There, folk music was transformed, ideas like racial equality and grassroots politics got their start, and the antiwar movement exploded. Prominent intellectuals, writers, poets, and musicians mingled with students and academics in the bars and coffee houses of Dinkytown. People had the opportunity to recreate who they were. Not only did Bob Dylan begin his journey there; it's also where community food co-ops and the introduction of Eastern philosophies found their origins. And Loyce Houlton, my favorite choreographer, got her start there too at the Oliver Baptist Church. She invented her own technique by blending and merging classical ballet and modern dance to create incredible spiritual and intellectual pieces like the *Nutcracker Fantasy* and *Carmina Burana.* Even the University of Minnesota's student-run station Radio K and *A Prairie Home Companion* with Garrison Keillor started in Dinkytown.

I grabbed the salad bowl (a wedding gift from my friend Maude of Dinkytown). It was filled with frisée lettuce, pickled pairs, blue cheese, and quail's eggs.

As I re-entered the room, Judy was talking. "My apartment was the central headquarters for everything. I had parties that didn't end until the next day. People would stop and unload everything on me. I remember the German girl…Ilka, or something like that, stopping by to tell me that she and Lawrence had slept at Maude's house," Judy said.

My eyes widened. "Maude! The good witch from the southeast. She's flying in to calm our spirits. But you mean Lawrence slept in her house without her knowing it?"

"Oh, poor Maude!" Andy blurted.

"Perhaps she knew and didn't care," Hughie observed.

"How do we always end up telling stories about Maude when we talk about Dinkytown?" I wondered.

"Maude *was* Dinkytown," Judy replied.

"Hughie, it was you who got me involved with her, but that project didn't turn out so well..." Andy trailed off.

"Sorry about all of that, but you were advertising it as such a good deal for a person like her. I trusted you," Hugh said quietly as if he didn't want the rest of us to hear.

Then Judy interrupted, perhaps trying to change the subject, "Hey guys, I didn't finish my story. Then Lawrence stopped by my apartment to tell me how guilty he felt for spending the night at Maude's when he knew it was against her rules."

"That's funny! Well, we all loved her and respected her anyway. Boy, I had no clue all of that was going on! I had to keep my nose in the books. Judy, celebrating your birthday makes me think of Maude's birthday. Hers was on the 15th of February. She used to say she missed Valentine's by a day. I wonder if that's why she never found love. Or perhaps she started saying that after she gave up looking for love…" I commented as I set the salad on the table, encouraging everyone to dig in.

"It's amazing that we always return to Maude," Judy said.

"Yes, she has such staying power! Don't you think? I wonder if people would like some more Maude stories?" I asked.

Then Hughie chimed in, "She was so maudlin and demure, a kind of shrink for all you transients"

Judy quickly retorted, "Oh my! Where do you even find those words? 'Maudlin'? And why were we transients?"

"Of course, you were transients! You'd stay at Maude's one night, then be out the next.... And Maude was the epitome of maudlin," he emphasized.

"She came from a very well-to-do family—she even went to finishing school—but she ended living in that basement anyway," I explained.

Hughie added, "When I was at Lindquist & Vennum I was working on a case and somehow the Hart Lumber Company came up. That was Maude's family's company. In the 1930s they were owed a lot of money, but nobody had any and so they finally went broke."

Andy made his not-that-funny joke. "Why did she decide to live in the basement? Did she like listening to all the junk flowing down the exposed sewer pipes?"

Then Judy added her two bits to try to be equally funny, "Maybe she liked looking at the tires of the cars parked outside and the legs and feet of people walking by. There were only two windows on the east side, but outside those windows, all Dinkytown's hubbub and weirdness was on display."

"Well," I said, "She grew some plants in those windows anyway."

Then Hughie added, "Maybe it was a business decision. She wanted to maximize tenancy."

Then I added another defense for her basement living, "Maybe it was her security and comfort. She was a sentimental pack rat. She had things hanging from the pipes, from lights from hooks to the max. Mementos of family and people she loved. That basement was her cocoon. A bomb could have blasted upstairs, and she wouldn't have known it.

Andy added his funny remark, "It was more of a cellar than a basement."

"But she had everything, even a unique wine bottle opener. After all that's how you met her, Elli," Judy added.

I had to come to Maude's defense again. "The space was all her own. The only thing she shared with tenants was the fridge, and the kitchen which was sectioned out in the boiler room."

"Remember that narrow dark closet where she hid her booze?" Hughie chimed in.

Andy chuckled and said, "I can still hear Hughie demanding some special Scotch on the spot."

"And she had it! I asked for Johny Walker, and she produced Chivas," he retorted.

Judy raised her glass and said, "More wine please! I want to ask you a question, Elli. Why were you so taken by her? What did you see in all that old junk and those old stories?"

Hughie's eyes glittered; he saw an opportunity to tease me,

"Oh yes Judy, you said it right: old. Elli loves old, the more ancient the better. She should've majored in archeology instead of engineering."

I had to say something. "Yes, her things were old, but they certainly weren't junk. Maude was no shrinking violet either. She would keep up with all the new trends and fashions. Remember when she gave up her Neiman Marcus designer shoes for Earth Shoes? And don't forget that she gave Hughie a lifetime subscription to *Playboy* for his birthday!"

"What? How? And why? Did she call it in?" Judy screamed with amusement.

I calmly explained to her, "She asked me what Hugh would like for a birthday present. I wouldn't answer. But she persisted, asking me what he liked. So, being kind of a jokester, I told her, 'A subscription to *Playboy* magazine.' She didn't even bat an eye… she said that she knew there were some good articles in it. Hughie received those magazines for twenty-five years."

"Unbelievable, you never told me that! She was too old! A spinster," she protested.

"She wasn't a spinster in the typical sense, and not really that old either. She was young at heart. Say whatever you want about her, but to me she was kind of a sage, a soul doctor. As I got to know her better, she became more of a puzzle that I wanted to solve."

Then Hugh stepped in to save the day. "We're just teasing you darling. Don't take it too seriously. Hey, let's raise our glasses to Maude and to Judy who introduced us. Happy Birthday, Judy!"

"It was her good luck she met you too, because you stood by her to the end," Judy said seriously.

And I concluded the Maude discussion saying, "She influenced all our lives in her own way and influenced all those who encountered her too. She became my family here. Alongside my grandparents, she lives in a special place in my heart."

Chapter 1

For the past forty years, every time I would drive down 4th St. S.E. near the University of Minnesota in Dinkytown, I wanted to stop at 1018; the old colonial house with the white Corinthian columns that had stood there since before the 1930s, full of dignity and grace. I wanted to pull in the gravel driveway and park, then walk to the side door and go down the basement stairs and call for Maude. I wanted to pour myself a cup of coffee, flop into the old wicker chair with the dampish pillow and wait for her to join me. Then I would tell her my latest news: my worries, thoughts, and petty problems; she would listen, as she always did, without comment or criticism, but with acceptance and a promise in her eyes that what I told her would not go beyond the four walls of her basement kitchen.

Every time I went past her house I felt as if I was passing a church after confession, a shelter of secrets, sorrows, and happy moments. I felt like I was holding communion with my past and at the same time I was experiencing the void of the absence left by my friend Maude.

Maude's House

I first met Maude in 1969. I was finishing my degree in Physics. I had come to the US from Greece as a Fulbright Scholar. I had to convince my family to let me study in the US. Even though my mother had won a scholarship to Smith College, my grandparents would not allow her to go to the US. Perhaps that made her more willing to let me go. I was frustrated by the education system in Greece and the constant political strikes. During my four years at university, I had focused on my studies and worked hard so I could complete my degree and return to Greece.

1969 was an important year for me. It was the year I met my closest friends: Judy, Maude, and my future husband Hugh. I remember it was a Friday afternoon in January. I had stopped over at Judy's, a newly acquired friend, who lived in Dinkytown by the University of Minnesota. I had brought a bottle of wine to celebrate the completion of one of the three term papers I had to write before I graduated. Judy had just moved into her new apartment and was painting her living room. She welcomed me as a relief from the work, and we both started sifting through her cardboard boxes, looking for a wine opener.

"I don't know where the heck anything is," she said with a frown. "Why don't you use a knife?"

"A knife!" I exclaimed. "It's a good wine. That will wreck it. We've got to have a wine opener. I think I'll walk down to Gray's Drug and see if I can find one."

Gray's Campus Drug, 1974

"Wait a second," she said. "You won't find a bottle opener at Gray's. Now let me think… I know! Go down to Maude's, she has a bottle opener."

"Maude's?" I asked. "Where's that?"

"Oh, Maude is a person. Sweet old Maude. That's where I lived when I was going to the U. You must meet Maude. You'll just love her."

"Go down 4th Street to 1018, it's the white house with the columns. She'll be there, she always is. If she doesn't answer, go to the side door, it's always open."

I hesitated. "Go, go," she insisted. "I'm ready for some wine."

I threw my coat on and walked down 4th Street. It was just beginning to get dark. The cloudless January sky had an ethereal rose quality. The elm trees, taupe and grey, had charcoal pink outlines. The details on the houses were beginning to fade and some lights were being turned on. The smokestacks rose in vertical, frozen columns. It was fifteen below. The snow, splattered with sand and salt, was piled in permanent hills along the streets and sidewalks. People and cars moved quickly by. I walked past a stalled car with its emergency lights on and hood open.

I looked across the street. There was the house, with four Corinthian columns. The number on the door said 1018 and there was a sign hanging in the window that read "Room for Rent." I crossed the street, went to the door and rang the bell. I waited for a while before I rang the bell again. I moved my feet up and down to get warm and raised my collar.

My breath was coming out in puffs and freezing around my scarf. I got antsy and opened the storm door. I started banging the door knocker and tried to peer through the leaded glass window. I could see an old-fashioned candlelight sconce on the wall and below a mahogany side table and the figure of somebody coming down the hall. I could only see the top of someone's head. It appeared to be a short person. As the figure came closer, a woman with a round face with glasses and curly hair came into focus looking up at me through the frosted window.

"Who is it?" she asked.

"It's Elli. I'm Judy's friend. I came to borrow a wine bottle opener, if you have one."

I heard her unchain and unlock the door.

She wore a smile. She had a stubby nose, hair tinted red, and a frail body that was stooped over a little. She was older, but of an undetermined age. She had on a print cashmere sweater with pearl buttons and another heavier sweater over it, a narrow black skirt, and black and rust designer shoes.

"Come on in," she said. "I'm Maude Hart."

"I'm glad to meet you. My friend Judy can't find her wine bottle opener. She was sure that you'd have one."

"Oh, you're Judy's friend. She used to live here. Certainly, I have a wine opener," she assured me. "Come on downstairs."

I checked the place out as I followed her. The stairs to the right went up. The living room on the left had massive antique mahogany furniture. The hardwood floors were completely covered with oriental rugs. A couple of the coffee tables were covered with rugs as well. We went past a side door and down a dark stairway.

At the bottom of the stairs there was a drape that was tied to one side. We went through another set of faded linen drapes into a long narrow room that looked like someone's living room. Two armchairs covered with crocheted Afghans sat in front of a large television. Between them was a cedar chest with trays full of buttons, pins, change, mail, papers, and other assorted junk. A beautiful Tiffany lamp with red tulips sat on top of it. A heavy silver tray with an oriental flower design rested on top of a mahogany stand (which served as a coffee table). Hanging from lamps and water pipes were red and green strips of remnant material which held scissors, keys, and tools. Along the north side of the room underneath small heavily draped basement windows there was a bed covered with a green velvet quilt, just visible through a sort of dark haze. Hanging over the bed there were many pictures: of a middle-aged businessman, of groups of smiling plump women in twenties outfits, and of the house alongside a drawing of a coat of arms titled "Hart."

White metal cabinets hung along the south side of the room. Two different remnant carpet pieces covered the cement floors and oriental rugs were scattered over them.

I followed Maude into a different room. It was an improvised kitchen in the furnace room with painted plywood panels sectioning out the furnace. The cupboards were asymmetrical and the countertops made of linoleum. There was a big white Hotpoint double oven and cooktop on one side of the room. The white enamel sink was across from it. A tattered oriental rug in front of the sink covered a worn-out spot on the linoleum floor. Through the window over the sink, I could see the tires of a car and the boots and pant cuffs of a guy climbing into it.

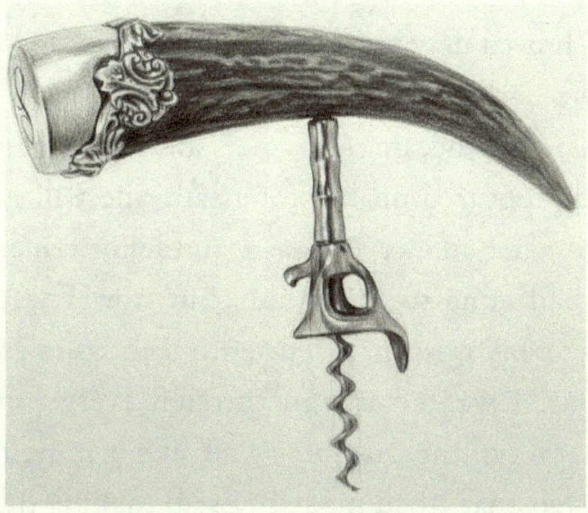

"Here it is," she said softly and turned my attention to the three-tiered rack over the kitchen table where the bottle opener hung along with embroidered kitchen towels and all kinds of other kitchen utensils. Carefully arranged on the shelf above sat cream-colored pottery with red, green, and blue heart and house designs that said: "Home is where the Heart is."

I suddenly felt that she was noticing that I was staring. I couldn't stop myself from asking, "Who lives down here?"

"Well, I do, and the girls have the privilege of the kitchen," she answered.

"Quite a privilege," I thought and suddenly, I got this urge to know more about her. "How long have you lived here?"

She looked surprised but she answered. "Oh, for ages, since the forties..."

"And you've always stayed down in the basement?"

"I moved down here when Father died and the servants left, back towards the end of World War II."

Her face became sad, her smile was gone, and wrinkles appeared on her forehead. She still held the bottle opener in her hands. I suddenly remembered why I had gone to her house, but now I wanted to stay there, my mission forgotten. I wanted to ask more questions. I wanted to run through every room and look at everything, explore it all like a museum. Because I felt that I had made her sad, making her travel to the past and talk about all those loved ones who weren't around anymore. I wanted to change that. Then I had an inspiration.

"Maude, you must have a vacancy here, since you've got your sign up. I currently live in Kenwood, but I'd rather be closer to campus."

Her well-preserved face lit up. It seemed like she saw dollar signs.

"It's the big room at the top of the stairs. The girl who lived there got married at Christmas. Everyone who stays there gets married and it's $55 a month and I'll show it to you," she said all in one breath. She was so excited that she ran all the words together without stopping.

She started walking towards the stairway and I followed her as I explained how I could move from Kenwood so fast.

"In my rooming house in Kenwood, I only have to give my landlady a week's notice. And the landlady doesn't like me that much anyway."

Upstairs she opened the door to the room that was available. It was huge and painted olive green. Two windows faced 4th Street, and the two windows showed a view of the fraternity next door. There was a bed, two maple chests, and faded linen drapes for doors. The hardwood floors were worn out and were slanting towards the outside of the house. It was an instant hit—I loved it!

"I'll take it."

"You will?" she said, so surprised that she dropped the bottle opener.

"Yes, I'll try to move in next Sunday, if that's okay with you," I replied as I picked up the bottle opener.

"It's okay with me, if it's okay with you," she said with a smile.

We walked downstairs. I was anxious to tell Judy. I looked at the wine opener. It was made with sterling and elk horn. It had a relief with the letter *H* on the handle.

"You may bring it back on Sunday," she told me.

"I certainly will," I assured her. "Bye for now, and thanks a lot."

"See you later," she said as she took down the "For Rent" sign from the window.

I walked back to Judy's. It was dark by then and all the cars had their lights on. The frosty air cooled my flushed face. I didn't know why I was so excited. Could it have been that she reminded me of my grandparents, who I revered? Was it my love of—almost obsession with—older people? Or it could have been the fascination with that old house, or perhaps the excitement of moving back closer to campus and my friend Judy.

Subconsciously though, I knew that I was intrigued with Maude. I was touched by her sadness when she thought of the past; but for sure it was her smile that warmed my heart and generated my unexpected affinity towards her. She also had a mysterious air about her that drew my curiosity and made me want to discover more about her. I just knew even then that she was going to become my best friend.

Chapter 2

I moved into Maude's the following Sunday evening. I arrived there with all of my belongings in a yellow cab. The room was clean and ready for me. She helped me settle in and took several trips from the basement to the third floor to bring anything I requested.

I unpacked my boxes, and she hung around listening to me talk. A couple of times she walked to the windows and pulled the drapes.

"The pharmacy fraternity guys over there like the action in this room, keep your drapes drawn," she warned me.

Later that night I realized that I had unloaded my life story onto her. I told her about my grandparents and my family, my boyfriends, and my academic studies. I found it easy to talk to her. The expression on her face showed me that she had listened very closely to everything I said.

That evening, I met Gloria, Mary, Debby, and Ilka. They all lived on the second floor, which was a veritable living organism, with telephones always ringing in the hall and girls buzzing back and forth, up and down. Each room was a story, and each story included a problem. The solver of those problems was Maude. As I lived there, I learned that the second floor was what made Maude timeless.

Her perfect lady manners, her strict rules about men in the house, her phobia (a remnant of the Depression era) of not having cash, her hiding of money and jewelry under mattresses and inside pillows, all mixed in a unique way with her progressive attitudes that were acquired over time from the young women who lived in the house. She was a liberal in politics, and a civil libertarian; she never missed a voting date.

A few years later I found out that one time she had walked through sleet and ice to go to the voting booth. I asked why in the world she would chance such weather for a vote. "We won this privilege," she said. "I will never give it up. It's noblesse oblige." That last statement took me by surprise.

"Noblesse oblige!" I exclaimed. "Where did you come up with that complex idea?"

"Well, I was born with it," she said quietly. In an instant she assumed a different status in my eyes. It had been a while since I had heard that phrase which frequently came up in my Greek family's discussions. Now, instead of thinking of my family discussions, I think of that phrase and of her every time I go to the voting booth. Noblesse oblige indeed, my dear friend Maude!

I have come to believe that noblesse oblige is genetic; some people have it, and others don't.

* * *

She loved gourmet food and recipes, designer shoes, and lacy underwear. She'd accept anything mod and far out that any of us would wear, and she would go as far as to tell us that she liked it.

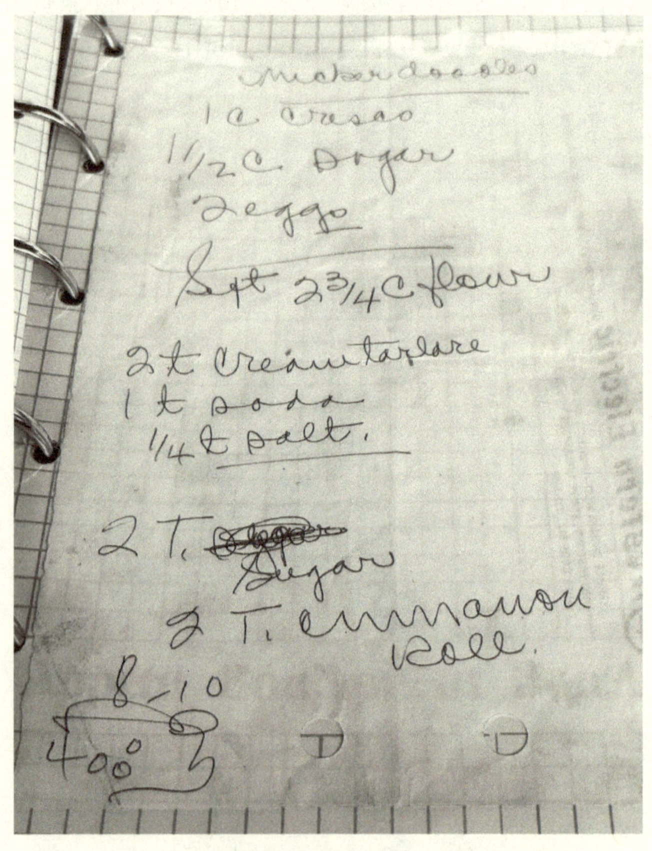

Maude's Handwritten Snickerdoodle Recipe

That winter and spring I got to know each of the other girls. They all had a relationship with Maude. They all respected her and liked her, some more than others, but the feelings were there.

Gloria was a lonely liberal arts student. She was in her senior year and was working hard on her degree. Her main endeavor, however, was developing her "intellectual" relationship with a priest.

"I love Maude," she'd say, "I love to sit down in the basement and talk to her. It's better than talking to my analyst. But I can never go as far as to tell her about my relationship with Father Jerome. I don't know that she'll understand."

So, I ended up learning a lot about Gloria's relationship with Father Jerome. I heard all about their secret retreats and trips, his tribulations about their relationship, and finally her disappointment when it all ended. She never breathed a word of it to Maude, but I had a feeling that Maude knew something all along. I remember her telling me casually, "Father Jerome stopped calling Gloria. He must have locked himself up in a monastery."

We all had to share one big bathroom upstairs. It was not exactly my favorite thing to do, but dorms weren't much better. Everyone was supposed to clean the bathtub drain, but some girls would forget. Gloria used to wash her underwear and hang it over the tub faucet to let it dry. I think they once were white but now they had a permanent grey tint. Debby used to complain when she found underwear over the faucet; she would grab them with a piece of toilet paper and hang them over a towel bar. Gloria never protested and sometimes she would thank Debby.

I took a disinfectant bottle and sprayed everywhere before I used the toilet and bathtub. I decided to cut my hair very short so it would be easier to wash.

Once Maude figured out I was a clean freak, she volunteered her big green bathroom on the main floor for me to use. I thanked her but declined. It was Maude's bathroom and none of us girls were going to invade it.

Maude also knew all about Debby's affair with a seventy-year-old man, mainly because Debby chose to tell her all about it in full detail, even including how they chased each other nude around the bed.

"She loves hearing all my adventures," Debby would tell us, explaining what she had divulged to Maude. "She compares herself to my boyfriend. It excites her imagination. It turns her on."

I never believed that story for a second, mainly because Maude would invariably take some aspirin and disappear into the dark corner of her bed after Debby got done talking to her.

Mary was Maude's favorite. She worked as a nurse, and she was engaged to a doctor. She would take Maude shopping and run errands for her. She would always pay her on time, and she would bring her gifts of flowers, candy, and cheese. After she got married, she moved out of town, but she kept up her correspondence with Maude, and she always tried to stop and visit when she was in town.

Ilka was a foreign student from Germany. She spent most of her time studying. Her relationship with Maude was cordial and polite.

Ilka was a post-war baby. Sometimes we got caught up in conversations about World War II and what Hitler did to my home country of Greece, but we always ended them with hope for a new Europe. She drew comparisons between what the Nazis did back in the 30's and '40s with what the US was doing in Southeast Asia, especially Vietnam. She hung around with antiwar groups and even joined antiwar demonstrations. I never participated in any such happenings, mostly because of my aversion to crowds, but also because I didn't want to do anything to compromise my scholarships and my status as a foreign student.

Partly because just a year before, Greece had been taken over by a military junta. Intellectuals and politicians from the previous government were imprisoned or exiled. Even my own brother, a student at the Polytechnic Institute at the University of Athens, was in danger. I was worried about him and the rest of my family. My father had always been a fierce advocate for human rights, and my mother was well-known and respected for her work in social services. What if they were imprisoned, too?

Then I thought of my grandfather, who used to remind me that the Greeks had survived the Ottoman Empire. "We are an independent people who can survive anything," he would say. "We Hellenized all kinds of races, but the Turks proved to be very difficult." Ever since the time of Troy the Greeks made colonies and traveled all the way to England and around the Black Sea. They weren't occupying these places but spreading their culture. They were conquered by many leaders and ideas including the Romans, but were successful in Hellenizing them and even Hellenized Christianity.

But there were also rumors circulating among Greek students at the U of M that the US had helped the military junta overthrow the old government because it was too leftist and they wanted regime change. The US had hosted me for four years; I didn't want to believe that it would be a part of overthrowing the Greek government. Part of me was afraid of being imprisoned or sent back to Greece if I circulated the rumors and criticized the US. So I tried to keep my nose in my books and keep my mouth shut.

Ilka continued to invite me to join her in demonstrations and walks. She kept telling me that her parents had been complacent and that was what lead to Hitler coming to power. She didn't want to be complacent like them. I agreed with her ideas, but I never participated.

Ilka would join many of our parties at Judy's and at the Mixers and loved to go to the German Black Forest Café. She loved her beer.

There were other characters that floated around at Maude's. Margaret was a middle-aged spinster lady who permanently lived in the big room behind the living room on the main floor. She worked for the telephone company and was home mainly in the evenings and on weekends. She would always advise Maude what to do. Maude seemed to ignore all that Margaret had to say and do whatever she wanted. That irritated Margaret who would say to Maude at least once a day, "You never listen to me. Whatever I tell you, you do the opposite. I only tell you because I like you."

Maude later told me that Margaret wanted to boss her around. "I must let all that bossing go over my head. You must understand that she has no one else to boss, she's a lonely person. Ignoring her keeps the peace in my house."

Yvonne and Jane were Maude's friends: Maude babysat their children. Jane was the wife of a chemistry professor and Yvonne the wife of a doctor. Yvonne was from England and Maude was very fond of her and her little girl Francesca. Yvonne would take Maude on long shopping trips. Yvonne trusted Maude so much she would leave Francesca to spend the night with her.

Both Jane and Yvonne had issues with their marriages. Maude was very compassionate and understanding and felt that these women were not getting a fair deal.

Meanwhile, I got to know Maude better. I spent many of my study breaks in the basement drinking coffee and munching on things that she baked. Maude was quite the baker. She loved to call certain places and get recipes which she would immediately try. When I got stuck on some difficult spot in my papers and wouldn't take a break, Maude brought cookies and coffee up to my room.

Many times, Maude and I would make a trip up to the third floor of the house looking for an extra chair or table for my room. During such trips we would pass by a corner where Maude had gathered many of her private family things. She would say, "Those were Father's."

On one of these trips, I learned that the Hart Lumber Company originated in Aberdeen, South Dakota. The Harts lived there when Maude was little. She reminisced about Aberdeen with great nostalgia. As a matter of fact, her brother's widow still lived in Aberdeen and Maude would get gifts from her during Christmas and on her birthday. When we passed by these items, Maude would get exceptionally chatty. I learned how the Harts made their money in the lumber business and how their business went broke during the Depression. One time she opened a trunk and showed me a book. The title of the book was *Who's Who in the Northwest.* The book had a bookmark and when we opened it this is what I read:

O. E. Republican. Universalist. ...
Kenwood Parkway, Minneapolis, Minn.

HART, John Samuel.—President, J. S. ...
Lumber Company, 638 Security Bldg., Minneap...
President, Hart Lumber Company. Vice-P...
dent, Hollandsworth-Hart Lumber Comp...
Born near Clinton, Iowa, Dec. 10, 1863, son of H...
A. and Mary J. Hart. Educated: Public Scho...
Iowa; Commercial College, Iowa. Livestock ...
ness, 1884-1889; lumber business, 1889-1898; ...
into business for himself, 1898, and is now a...
member of several companies. Married ...
Maude Marshall, daughter of Clark T. Mar...
Charter Oak, Iowa, 1888; has one son and two da...
ters. Clubs: Interlachen; Minneapolis Ath...

So Maude was the princess-daughter of a Minnesota lumber baron. I learned about her Lake Minnetonka summer house and their Lake of the Isles winter home at 2501 Girard Avenue. She shared a few details about her sister Cloe and her marriage to a young businessman. She told me about their baby, and we flipped through albums. Maude's details were scant, and she would be silent for long periods. She said that her sister, her sister's husband, and the baby all died one after the other. Her father died of depression in 1945 after his business could not be resurrected. I saw her sadness taking over and promised to never ask her those questions again.

After her father died, Maude took a job as a salesgirl at the Dayton's department store. She took care of her mother who later died at a very old age. I learned that Maude had even gone to a girl's finishing school. However, at Dayton's she just worked as a salesgirl. Though she worked there as a full-time employee, Dayton's kept her hours low enough to pay her only $25 per month of pension, though Maude was not bitter about it. She used to subscribe to *The Daytonian* and she had some savings in the employee credit union.

I found out that Maude hated her only living relative in Minneapolis with a passion. She was suspicious of him and thought that he was after her house and property. She would get all worked up when he would call. On those rare occasions she would look for me afterwards and tell me about him.

"My cousin John Hart called again," she'd say. "I don't know what he wants. He asked me over for dinner. I don't know what gave him the idea that I'd want to have dinner with the likes of him and his ill-mannered children."

"Maude, come on." I would try to persuade her. "Maybe he wants to be friendly. Maybe you're not being fair to him."

"Sure, he wants to be friendly. He's after my property. Most likely he wants to poison me."

"Maude, that's quite the statement. What gave you that idea?"

"Idea!" she'd exclaim. "He's gone as far as to ask me if I had a will. I won't ever forgive him for that. I am a witch."

My suggestions to think rationally were of no use. Maude had made up her mind about her cousin, and she was not about to change it. Her comment about being a witch was a typical one. She'd use it often when she was mad about someone. She'd install faucets with automatic turnoffs in the main bathroom, so Margaret wouldn't use too much water. Or she'd give Debby a day's notice to move out or pay her rent and she would explain it all saying, "I've got to do that. I am a witch you know."

As I lived there longer, I got to know the house, every room and corner. Maude kept the living room on the main floor as a tribute to her parents. Everything inside was from Aberdeen. Maude would try to keep it clean and perfect, but all the beautiful old antique furniture still showed the marks of the boarders who had lived there.

On the main floor, besides Margaret's room there was also the "little room" which was kept vacant. It had been her mother's room until the day she died.

Maude's bathroom was the great big bathroom on the first floor. It had Williamsburg green fixtures and linoleum floors. The bathroom always smelled of sweet bubble bath and baby powder. It was Maude's favorite place to retreat after a hard day of getting a room ready for a new tenant. She'd disappear in there for hours, perhaps contemplating the gold framed verse that hung on the wall opposite the tub:

My dear one
I wish you were here
You left my heart alone
I can't stop thinking of thee

I often wanted to ask Maude about that verse, and if it was about someone in particular. But as I learned more about her past, I began to feel that the verse was really about everyone she had ever loved.

Once when we were talking about her sister, she said to me, "Cloe was the pretty one in our family. I was short and homely, especially after my nose was broken in an accident. I had my chances though, that's it. I had my chances."

After saying that, her face would get solemn and vague. She became suspended in the past and its melancholy. Many times, she'd get that look when we would go to the third floor looking for something. She'd ask me to go up to help her move a table or rug, and then we'd stumble across something that would make her gloomy and silent.

The third floor also held the stories of past roomers. It was the cemetery of all the belongings that they had left behind: Angelique's hats still in boxes from the '40s, mahogany chests painted pink by Leona, who loved pink and lived there in '54, wigs from Dorothea. Bikes, books, boxes of fabrics and clothes, shoes, rugs, radiators covered with drapes, and most certainly mattresses. Oh! All those stained mattresses; the girls never took care of them during their time of the month.

Deeper in the attic, as I had seen before, were the remnants of the Hart family business. There were desktops and walnut doors and cabinets from her father's office. There were even boxes of their accounting books.

Maude's basement was her present, although it was surrounded by pictures and memories of the past. It was her sanctuary, the territory of her absolute reign. Her kitchen sparked Maude's gourmet creativity, making her the best cook southwest of Dinkytown. After all, she was a subscriber to *Gourmet* magazine.

The shoe boxes on top of her cedar chest served as the ideal filing spot for all her receipts and IOU's. The metal cabinets in the living room were all full of the family's Limoges china and cut crystal. Perhaps Maude felt that she guarded it all by sleeping in her basement. She didn't want it stolen, but oddly at the same time she was very generous and ready to give it to you if she liked you and if she felt that you would appreciate whatever it was.

There was one more room in the basement which she called "her room." The door was usually shut. There, the closets, the dressing tables, and the bed all faded in the dark. There, as I found out later, the secrets of her girlhood were kept, moist from a combination of tears and years of basement mustiness.

She just loved that basement. Come winter or spring, you'd find her down there baking or sewing or sifting through papers and bills. The coffee was always ready, and the caramel rolls were in the warmer, and she used to love to bring out the Chivas Regal (for those of us who knew that she drank).

CHAPTER 3

It was during the winter and spring of 1969 when I started to date Hugh. Maude had made me appreciate his tweed jackets, bow ties, camel hair coat, sense of humor, and the sparkle he got in his eyes when he teased her.

"He comes from very good stock," she'd tell me repeatedly. "He was born in a cashmere jacket. There are not many men who can wear a bow tie the way he does, and it's a real one. I can just see him in court All he'd have to do is just stand there and he'd win any case."

All Hugh had to do was just stand there to win Maude's heart, as well as mine.

Sometimes Hugh would stop by 1018 unannounced, ring the doorbell, then sit in a chair and wait to see who would open the door. It usually happened late in the afternoon when his classes were over and before he went into his evening study sessions. Sometimes he would be finishing an ice-cream cone that he had picked up at

Bridgeman's on his way over. Usually someone would open the door and call me down. Sometimes it would be Maude who was always excited to see him and would invite him into her mahogany-furnished living room before calling me down.

Bridgeman's Ice Cream, 1974

Sometimes she would hang around waiting to be invited into our conversation, which happened nine out of ten times. We had some very interesting conversations together ranging from issues like politics to issues that the city of Minneapolis was dealing with to personal issues.

Maude wanted to be certain that the person who was invited in to sit in her mahogany chairs was worthy of it. She knew all about Hugh's family's business as they were an old Minneapolis company.

Hugh did not mind her participation in these conversations, and I certainly enjoyed learning more about him and things that I would have been reluctant to ask him myself. During one of these conversations, I learned about his love of motorcycles and his motorcycle adventures.

Because Maude had a different appreciation for Hugh's family business, one day she asked him point-blank, "How come you're not going to work for the family business and are studying law instead?"

Hugh smiled but was unperturbed. He answered her, "My father felt that the best requirement for a good businessman is the thorough understanding of the law, so I have to know the law to be involved in the family business, if I ever do, and, and…"

He stopped talking as if he felt that his answer was getting too long and a bit complicated.

Now he had piqued my curiosity. "And, and?" I pressed.

"Oh, do you really want to know? My answer might be a good introduction to our American political system, for a foreign student…" he said.

"Come on, spit it out! I can learn, and Maude most likely already knows about it," I encouraged him.

"Well in the US of A, we are not governed by a ruler, a king, a dictator, or a political party. We are not a theocracy. We have our constitution and the most incredible system of laws…" He answered in one breath and then continued, "Before I decided to study US law and go to school for it, I rode more than 2,500 miles around Europe and even ended up in an East Berlin jail. It made me realize I'm proud of our law, our constitution, and our style of government."

Maude was grinning from ear to ear and I thought that she was going to jump up and kiss him.

American nationalism, I thought and quickly tried to change the subject. "You said you rode. Were you on bike?"

"Indeed, I was," he answered.

So that's how Maude and I found out about Hugh's love of motorcycles and some of his motorcycle adventures. We both concluded that he was kind of a daredevil. We also learned about his love for the machines and the fact that he knew how to fix them.

Maude and I discussed him afterwards. Down in her basement, she over a glass of scotch and me over some port, we analyzed all he said and concluded that he was an intelligent and honorable person, a brave, fair, and balanced man.

***

After finishing my final papers and graduating, I signed up for graduate school and decided to take the month of August to return home. I paid Maude for August and September and asked her not to rent my room to anyone else.

As I was leaving for the airport, Maude ran after me and gave me a card. She wished me happy and safe travels. It made me tear up; it was a blessing, and I've kept it safe up to this day. Now that all those who gave me blessings are gone, I look at it and hope that these blessings will last me for my whole life's journey.

Things changed for me that August. Hugh was going around the world after passing the bar exam. He stopped over to visit me in Greece in the same nonchalant fashion he walked to 1018 from Bridgeman's. In his usual charming way, he won my mother's and all my family's hearts. His whole family ended up coming over from Minnesota to visit.

Our families hit it off. It turns out that culture, especially European, can flow easily across the ocean. We spoke with a mix of Greek, French, and English. As a matter of fact, I hadn't heard this much French spoken since when I was little and my mother and aunt spoke to each other in French so we wouldn't understand. Quotes from Shakespeare to Balzac; verses from Kavafis to Lamartine; and Greek proverbs ancient to modern flew between us all. Each member of my family and his felt appreciated and understood by the others.

We were married in Greece and returned to Minnesota in September. Despite their congeniality towards Hugh and his family, my family wasn't too happy about my leaving again. They felt that four years apart was enough. But Hugh had an important job waiting for him, so he promised my mother he would send me home every summer.

The last time I talked to Gloria, Debby, and Ilka was at the party Hugh and I had after our wedding. All three of them moved out of Maude's either because they had graduated or because they got engaged. New girls moved in, and I didn't get to know them as well. I continued my friendship with Maude, however, and somehow it became stronger.

Then it was my turn to leave. I moved my things out of Maude's in Hugh's mother's yellow Buick convertible. We were to live in the town of Excelsior. The far distance between us didn't keep me away from Maude. Dinkytown was only just a breeze away. I visited her very often and I talked to her on the phone every day. She became my confidant in matters of in-law relationships and my advisor in matters of cooking and baking. She also shared with me some of her moral convictions and personal cultural beliefs. In both these areas we found common ground and connections.

Many times our trips took us to the Goodwill where Maude would search for cashmere sweaters, and I would look for antiques. We always came out with a couple of treasures and some memorable encounters with other customers. On one of our trips, we were waiting in the checkout line when a well-dressed woman stormed to the front of the line demanding the clerk's attention. She was carrying a big cardboard box which she set on the counter. We waved her ahead of us. She wanted to see if she could get some money for or donate what she had in the box. The clerk called in another person to evaluate. Out of the box came the most beautifully starched and ironed linen placemats and tabletop covers.

"Please," she said, "my mother spent all her time keeping these things in top shape. Don't know why in the heck she didn't turn them into dish rags. Her house is filled with all this junk. Someone told me that I could get rid of them at the Goodwill. Can I?"

Maude was silent and so was I. We did not see those items as junk. The woman negotiated with the cashier and left the box there. Then she vanished as fast as she had appeared.

We were next in line. Maude bought her sweater and then turned to me and said, "Check out the box. Perhaps there are some treasures there."

So I did.

Besides the most beautiful placemats and napkins there were some other things that I didn't recognize. Little square and round envelopes that perhaps could hold something. Maude explained to me that these items were made for insulating pads of hot dishes so that they could be set on a table without damaging it.

Maude and I discussed how beautiful the woman's mother's dining table would have been, set with items like that.

I offered them $50 for the box. Goodwill happily took it.

Maude had a smile on her face. On the way back to her house, we had a very interesting conversation.

"This is something her mother loved for a lifetime. She shouldn't have dashed it off with such fury."

"Yes," I said, "my grandmothers spent lifetimes embroidering and needlepointing. I have never thrown anything of theirs away. And what I bought here will grace my dinner parties."

"This woman's mother is kissing you from the sky. That woman had no respect for her mother's life."

"Yes, but why do you suppose she said that her mother spent all her time keeping 'those things' in top shape? What else did she want her mother to do?"

"Then she said that her mother should have turned them into dish rags. Why didn't she turn them into dish rags herself? And she went out of her way to bring them to the Goodwill."

"How could you figure this one out? She must have been a tough one to raise," Maude replied. "Oh well, I guess people don't have time to wash and iron any more, plastic and paper is everywhere. That said, she could have kept a couple and framed them, or whatever. They're a piece of art, and women created them," I said.

"I gave my mother's embroidery to Mary when she got married and she loved them. She was that kind of person."

Maude had held incredible respect for her parents. She revered her father and loved her mother and the gentle and sophisticated way they lived. I grew up among people like her and her family. Though my family had lost a lot of their belongings and estates because of war and catastrophe, they took good care of what they had. Maude hadn't experienced the level of catastrophe my family had—the Greek genocide in Asia Minor, the German occupation and the looting and destruction of property—however, she had experienced the Great Depression and the end of her family's business. She respected and treasured the belongings she still had and honored her parents' traditions and was proud to talk about them. The specific circumstances were different, but they left us both changed with the epigenetic forces of those traumas. Despite this we both held onto our family's values of respect and honor.

***

We also took trips to the Lyndale fruit and flower market so we could buy the best peaches available, and we would split the case. Maude would make upside down peach cake, and I would eat peaches for a week straight.

Then, there was rhubarb. We had to go to the Minneapolis farmers market for that. We had to inspect all the rhubarb to find the one with the right quality.

"Come on Maude, rhubarb is rhubarb," I would say.

"No, my dear, it has to be the right color and crispness," she would answer.

Rhubarb Cake

- ½ cup shortening (half butter)
- 2 cups brown sugar
- 2 eggs
- 2 cups flour
- 1 tsp. soda
- Salt, dash
- 1 cup buttermilk
- 1 tsp. vanilla
- 1½ cups rhubarb, cut small
- ¼ cup white sugar
- 1 tsp. cinnamon

Cream together shortening and brown sugar. Add eggs and beat. Sift flour with soda and salt and add alternately with buttermilk. Add vanilla. Fold in rhubarb. Pour in greased and floured 9 x 13 pan. Top cake with mixture of white sugar and cinnamon. Bake at 350° for 40 to 50 min. Serves 12 or more.

Maude's Rhubarb Cake Recipe

Dilly Bread

1 cup cottage cheese
1 pkg. yeast, dissolved in ¼ cup warm water
2 tbsp. sugar
1 tbsp. butter
1 tbsp. instant onion
2 tbsp. dill seed or weed
1 tsp. salt
¼ tsp. soda
2½ cups flour
1 egg, unbeaten

Heat cottage cheese until lukewarm. Add sugar, butter, onion, dill, salt, soda, yeast, egg. Mix together, then add flour. Let rise until double. Put into well-greased, 1½-qt. casserole. Bake at 350° for 45 to 50 min. 1 loaf.

Maude's Dilly Bread Recipe

She was also crazy about dill. She made the best dilly bread. Once she gave me a cookbook that had both the rhubarb cake and the dill bread recipe. After all these years this cookbook still has a special spot in my kitchen.

Maude felt good because it was empowering to have someone ask for her advice and listen to her, even if it was just for recipes.

"When you get to a certain age, things are not right with your body and then people no longer have a use for you." She said to me one day, "But you aren't like all those other people."

We had many Christmases and Thanksgivings together, and since my family was on the other side of the Atlantic, all our friends and Hugh's family accepted Maude as my closest immediate relative.

Maude always came with a gift for the hostess: she would dig into her inventory of things she had amassed through the ages and always produce something special that she appreciated herself: sometimes it would be a Limoges bowl, a Japanese hand painted demitasse, or a cut crystal vase. Some pieces were especially beautiful and still adorn my houses. To this day, there is a Maude chair in Arizona and a Maude desk at my guest house. The beautiful Hart Lumber Company notary seal still sits on Hugh's desk. Sometimes things she gave me were broken or chipped and they ended up in our attic.

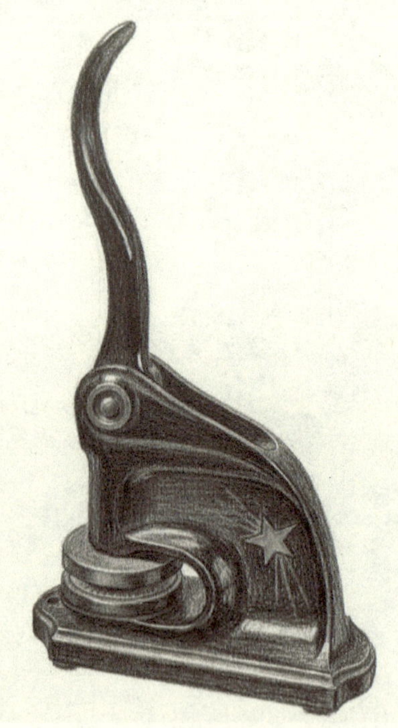

I specifically recall one time I visited, when she guided me to the basement window and pulled the dark faded curtain aside to reveal a beautiful porcelain vase with a girl holding a rose. The light from the window was dim. She stood up on her tippy toes and brought it down and set it on the kitchen table. The kitchen glittered from the light falling on the vase's gold leaf making the beautiful girl with the red hair even more magnificent, and even giving the old, chipped enamel sink an uplift. It was in perfect shape.

"Here, take this," she said.

"Why, don't you want it?" I asked.

"No," she said. "It makes my teeth itch."

So now this porcelain urn is sitting in my living room alongside her little serving tray, where the Limoges demitasse cups are displayed together with those from Hugh's grandmothers.

Another time she brought over a crystal bottle. "Kingsley Murphy gave this to my mother. It was bottle of Chanel No. 5, perhaps you have a use for it?"

"Who was Kingsley Murphy?" I asked.

"Oh, they were the Minneapolis paper people. Very important family and still at it."

* * *

Meanwhile things were changing at Maude's house. Girls moved in and out. Her relationship with Yvonne changed as well. Yvonne was going through a nasty divorce, and she spent a lot of time with Maude. She almost moved into Maude's house. Maude learned to love and have compassion for Yvonne and Francesca, and she learned to hate Yvonne's husband. She hated him almost more than Yvonne did, and had Yvonne not moved out of town, Maude could have ended up hating the whole male species, because of Yvonne's divorce.

Hughie was always the exception. He was her favorite person and not the low caliber of those other males. Maude wanted to take care of Yvonne and Francesca. It was not until a long time later that I realized that Yvonne was using and taking advantage of Maude. Without my knowledge, she had manipulated Maude into writing a new will and leaving everything to her.

When Yvonne eventually got divorced and moved out of town, Maude and I became even closer friends. I would take her shopping on expeditions to the Salvation Army where she would hunt for sweaters and antiques.

I would bring her fruits, vegetables, and goodies that she could not get elsewhere. I would stop before work and have coffee with her down in the basement and Hugh and I would stop for a drink there before a concert. She'd sit Hugh in the big papa chair and bring him a drink of Scotch. On the way out she would send him home with some of her famous peanut butter cookies. I still have the recipe.

PEANUT BUTTER COOKIES

1 cup butter	2 beaten eggs
1 cup peanut butter	2 tsp. soda
1/2 cup white sugar	2 cups flour (sifted)
1/2 cup brown sugar	2 cans salted peanuts

Mix butters, sugars, and eggs. Add soda, flour, and peanuts. Mix. Roll into small balls and place on greased cooky sheet. Flatten with fork. Bake about 10 minutes in 375 degree oven. If you do not add peanuts, add 1/4 tsp. salt.

Maude's Peanut Butter Cookies Recipe

Hugh and Maude

During these visits, Hugh amused himself with all the things that hung from the ceiling and the walls. One evening he discovered the Hart coat of arms that hung on the wall near the corner of her bed.

"Maude, now what's this Hart insignia on your wall?" he asked her.

"Oh, that's an old story."

"Come on Maude, tell me where you found this," he insisted.

Maude smiled as if she knew something special.

"Do you really want to know?"

"I sure do. Come on, tell me."

Maude disappeared into the basement closet. For a while we thought that she'd never come out. Then she reappeared holding a carefully wrapped scroll in her hands. It was tied with a red silk ribbon.

"Here, read this," she said to Hugh, giving him the scroll.

"What is this Maude, the Ten Commandments?" Hugh asked teasingly.

He carefully untied the silk ribbon, made himself comfortable by the Tiffany lamp, and started reading.

"I, the undersigned, swear that..."

Then, he stopped reading out loud, but his eyes were laughing, and he was trying to hide a smile.

"And how much did you have to pay for this?" Hugh cross-examined Maude.

"Well fifty dollars, plus." She said with reluctance. "What do you think of it?" she asked as she poured some Scotch into his glass.

"It's quite the document!" he said, concealing his smile by chewing some ice from his drink. Then he handed the scroll over to me.

As I read, I realized that what the document said was that the person who sent the document swore that he copied word for word all of the above, which was not at all about the Harts but about the O'Harts. Then it was signed and sealed with three different colored seals and was sold for fifty dollars and shipped to Maude, together with the coat of arms.

* * *

We drove home quietly that evening. We wanted to laugh but felt more like crying. She was still so in love with the status and importance of her family; over time though depression can bring a person down and it can become hard to hold onto the dignity of who you once were.

Another time we stopped by after a Law School event. We rolled down the back stairs and Hughie found his Big Papa chair and demanded his drink. Maude vanished into the closet and reappeared holding a big bottle of Chivas and a big smile.

"Now Maude," said Hughie, "Prohibition is over, you don't have to hide your booze. Perhaps you don't remember Prohibition? Were you old enough to know what it was?"

"Ha," she said, "that is the $64,000 question. Do I remember Prohibition? Do I remember all the crazies who were supposed to give us morals and religion?"

"What *is* the $64,000 question?" I asked.

"Tell you later," Hughie said. "Let Maude tell us about the crazies."

"I don't want to remember…" Maude said. "Where do I begin? It was at a time when a person was considered bad for not going to church on Sunday and instead driving his car to Lake Minnetonka. Father did not care. He was not influenced by all the religious talk and all the fanatics. We would all get into his convertible, and he would drive us all to our house at Lake Minnetonka. We had such a great time especially in the summer and fall. I never learned how to drive but I did not need to. Then there were those crazies complaining about the kind of science kids were being taught in school. And more, and most importantly, some small-time lawyer from Minnesota introduced that stupid amendment and his Volstead Act rule of what was intoxicating. And then a civil war started. Our country became ruled by criminals and gangsters."

"Wow, Maude!" Hugh said. "That was a mouthful. You summarized an entire era in US history, I'm impressed!"

So, Maude lived through Prohibition, and the Scopes trial, and the gangster gangs that ruled Minnesota and the $64,000 question. *The $64,000-Question* was a prime TV game show in the '50s—as was explained to me. So, in one breath she went from the twenties to the sixties at light speed. It was time travel extraordinaire!

We had more than one drink at Maude's basement that night. "We never were out of liquor," she said.

* * *

One morning I stopped at Maude's for coffee and started telling her about some formal event I had to attend in a couple of days. Maude quickly stood up and ran out of the kitchen. I thought she was going to run to the bathroom and be back. I waited for a while and then went looking for her because I needed to leave for work.

"Maude, where did you go?" I called.

I saw her emerging out of her deep dark bedroom holding a hat box. "What have you got there, Maude?" I asked, looking at the faded wooden hat box.

"Oh, just something for you to wear to your reception event," she said as she tried to open the box.

"Yes! What is it?" I asked.

Out of the box came a black hat with a little veil and then another squished one.

"Oh, Maude," I said, "these are cool. When did you wear these? They look like hats from the '20s." I couldn't help but think they looked like clothes straight out of *The Great Gatsby.*

"You are right. Some marvelous time in the past when I felt very fashionable."

"Let me go to work now and I will be back later on today to take them, then you can tell me exactly when it was that you were so fashionable."

I ran out the door so I would not be late for work but returned later to find out more amazing things about my little old friend.

We sat at the kitchen table, but she quickly got up and said that we needed something to drink. She brought a bottle of Scotch and an old bottle of port that I had left there a long time ago.

"Good, you found my port," I said. "You know I have a fascination with that era, ever since my literature class, English 105. We spent most of the class studying F. Scott Fitzgerald. Our teacher was obsessed with him. So, I got hooked as well. I had forgotten all about it until you showed me that hat. Were you a flapper with bobbed hair and short skirts?"

"Oh well, those were some heady times, but I was never a part of those groups. We always listened to Father and wouldn't imagine ever embarrassing him."

"Did you go to parties and jazz concerts?"

"I hardly ever did, but my sister Cloe was the star. She wanted to be a Mrs. *Somebody* and have a Mr. Somebody rule her life…oh well."

Then I saw her face get sad, her eyes focusing on some distant time, just staring into space. I felt bad and didn't want to bring sad stories to the surface. I wanted to change the subject.

"Maude," I said. "Your favorite person is going to stop by for a Scotch. We're meeting some friends in Dinkytown tonight for dinner."

"You mean Hughie? Oh my, I better comb my hair." She stood up and almost ran to the upstairs bathroom.

I took the hats home and never mentioned the flappers and all that jazz again. It must have been another bittersweet chapter of her life.

As the years passed, Maude went through all kinds of crises, from leaky roofs to girls whose boyfriends would call and tell Maude that they had gotten venereal diseases from the girl living there.

The biggest crises were when it turned out that Maude's next-door neighbor from China, had been paying Maude's property taxes. When Maude discovered this, she panicked. She thought that the next-door neighbor—who was equally confused—was after her property. It all culminated in Hugh's office where it was resolved, much to Maude's relief.

She had arrived at Hugh's office in the IDS Center dressed in a black suit, wearing her little black hat and her black and orange designer shoes. She arrived an hour and a half before the meeting and Hugh entertained her by showing her around the office and teasing her; he took her to the telescope telling her that he could zoom in on her house and could see the neighbor moving her out. She got very upset, so Hugh had to fess up that he was just making that up and took her back to his office with a cup of coffee. He told her to relax until the neighbor and his lawyer arrived.

When he got back to his office, Maude quickly concealed her little bottle of B&B that she had brought along to boost her morale during the meeting. In the end, all was resolved and Hugh took Maude back to her house.

Many times, Yvonne would come from out of town and spend time with Maude. It was during one of those visits that she persuaded Maude to buy a small Yorkshire Terrier, since Yvonne had one as well. It was Valentine's Day when Puddings arrived in Maude's life, and they became inseparable.

Puddings ate meat, liver, and peas and she became so fat that she had a hard time breathing. Taking Puddings to the trimmers was a regular job and she became an indispensable guest at our Christmas and Thanksgiving dinners. Puddings would sit on Maude's lap and have little bites of food, drooling on top of my Fortuny covered chairs...all of it I overlooked for Maude's sake.

CHAPTER 4

The years slipped away, and I did not notice that Maude was really aging. I had never known how old she was, and she was not about to answer that question. I remember how surprised I was when I finally found out her age.

Maude had been complaining about her eye hurting her for a whole week. She was not the type of person that would complain about ill health, since she believed that she could cure almost anything with a good rub of Listerine.

After a few days of hearing her complain, I asked her if we should go to a doctor.

"No doctors," she said. "You know once they get you in their claws, it's the end."

Somehow, secretly, I had the same feelings about the medical profession as Maude, but I did not want to admit it to her.

"I have kept myself very healthy by not going to any of those people and I don't want to start now."

"Perhaps there is something in your eye," I said. "Besides, this doctor is a friend, he is fun. He even almost looks like you—why he could have been your child. He has curly hair and wears designer shoes."

So, I took her to Burnsville where a friend of mine had an eye clinic. That day we discovered that Maude had glaucoma. The main thing that bothered Maude, however, was that the registration nurse wanted to find out how old she was.

"Miss Hart," she asked Maude, "when is your birthdate?"

"My birthday is February 15," Maude replied emphatically.

"What year Miss Hart?" The nurse insisted.

Maude stood up from her chair, straightened out her little black hat and coat, and looked around. There were many people in the waiting room. They were all looking at Maude now. It looked as though they were all waiting to hear her age. Maude looked around once again.

"How old are you, Miss Hart?" the nurse insisted.

"Social security age," Maude replied in a loud voice. The faces around the room appeared surprised. Maude approached the desk where the nurse sat and said softly, "Plus ten more and another ten more..." I heard her and so did the nurse, but no other person heard. The secret was now out. That secret somehow started a change in Maude. It might also have been the fact that she finally had to go see the doctor.

During the winter of 1976, I was putting a lot of effort into my job. My frequent trips out of town as well as my social life made me neglect a lot of social duties, even writing to my mother. My telephone calls and visits to Maude also decreased. On her birthday, when I tried to call her and tell her that I was going to be over, I learned that she was very sick.

I found her in her old room in the basement, all curled up in a quilt. I persuaded her to move out of that room and into the bed that was in her basement living room. I promised her that I was going to clean everything up and that she could move back in.

Cleaning that room was an unforgettable experience. Puddings had gone to the bathroom everywhere. There were bags of underwear and clothes dating as far back as the 1920s. I found training bras and diaries, hankies with dead flowers inside them, a man's single glove, and a pair of studs tied together with a ribbon. I found articles and pictures of young men who died or got married. I found baby booties and a dried-up corsage.

I don't remember what I threw out and what I shoved in drawers. Maude sat in the chair and watched me. She did not have the energy to object to what I was doing. She sat in the chair with a far off look on her face.

I knew that she was not there with me. The damp and smelly basement, the old paraphernalia that I was going through, Maude sitting in that chair but being somewhere else; all of it made me feel like I was doing something wrong. I felt like I was raping her, violating her memories. After all, who was I? I thought of the warmth I felt when I was home in my room and with my family. Maude had no family. The objects from the past and this room must have provided that same warmth for her and here I was ripping it all apart. I felt guilty, but on the other hand I could not leave her to rot in that basement. I sat next to her and looked searchingly into her eyes. I put my arm around her hunched shoulders and tried to console her.

"Maude, you really have got to get better. You must get rid of this cold. I will clean up this room, and I will bring some paint over and paint it. We will fix things up for you so that they are better. We will ask one of the girls to take Puddings out to go potty. Trust me, I am your friend."

"I know you are my friend," she said. "But I am too tired... People are not the same anymore. They steal my furniture and my rugs."

I felt alone with her fear of death, with her fear that vultures were out there waiting to dive in. I had to get both of us out of that state of mind.

"Come on, Maude," I said. "You are a witch—be a witch. We've got to make things better."

Things did get better that spring. I took Maude to the University Family Practice Clinic. Her health did improve. The house got organized; I painted her basement. And my visits and calls became frequent again.

CHAPTER 5

In 1977 my son Ted was born. Maude loved him.

"I'm glad you had a boy," she would say many times. "It's a man's world out there. I wish I was born a man."

We visited her often and brought her and Puddings over for dinner. As my son grew, he learned to love Maude. He looked forward to our visits to the basement where there was an underground world of things hanging from the ceiling and overflowing out of boxes and cabinets; a world of strings, tools, buttons, and unfamiliar broken objects waiting to be touched and investigated by his little vibrating hands that could not decide what to investigate first. Maude had one of the girls go to Gray's and buy him a red toy car, but that would not distract him from all the wonderful things scattered around Maude's basement.

The summer when he was three, we went to Europe for a month. I felt confident that all was fine at Maude's. The roof of the house was fixed. The problems with the rainwater coming into the basement had also been fixed, and the girls who stayed at Maude's were halfway decent. Terry was a girl who had lived at Maude's in the past, and Maude liked her. She decided to live at Maude's again at that time.

When I came back from Europe, however, I found out that things had taken an unexpected turn. One of the girls who liked Maude had left messages on my answering machine for me to call her as soon as I got back. Her name was Diane. Diane's number was not the same as Maude's, which indicated to me that she had moved out. When I called Diane, I found out that Terry had moved all the girls out of Maude's and had moved her boyfriend in under the pretense that he was repairing the house. Diane told me that Terry was using Maude's credit cards and was taking money out of Maude's hiding places and her bank account.

I went to Maude's with Diane. The side door was locked and chained. We knocked and knocked for a long time. We could hear Puddings barking. Finally, we saw Maude dragging herself up the basement stairs. Maude was overjoyed to see us. She looked clean and well at first, but on closer inspection her eyes had a fearful look in them. She had a hard time walking and talking, too.

"Maude, you don't look too good," I said. "What's the matter? Why have all the girls moved out of the house?"

"There is nothing the matter. I just missed you, and my legs kind of hurt."

"Maude, what's going on? Why did Terry move her boyfriend in? What happened with your rule of no men in the house?"

"He stays on the second floor and is fixing the bathroom. Terry said that he is not her boyfriend, just a good craftsman."

Diane and I ran to the second floor. There were a lot of tools outside the bathroom, but no repairs were going on. Maude was still standing on the basement stair landing, holding onto the doorknob.

Puddings was licking something wet off the linoleum floor. Maude, seeing me stare, had to explain.

"I cannot control it anymore," she said, looking like she was about to start crying. "They threatened me that they were going to tell you."

"What did they want you to do, Maude?" Diane asked.

"They wanted me to change it," Maude said.

"To change what?" Diane insisted.

"The will, just the will," she said and tried to sit down on the floor. Diane and I held her at the elbows.

"You had a will?" I asked with surprise. Then realizing that the priority was to have Maude sit down, I said, "We'll help you go downstairs, and you can tell us all about it."

That day I learned that Maude had previously made a will leaving everything to Yvonne. She told us that she did not want to make that will, but she was forced to do it by Yvonne's attorney. I learned that Terry had found those documents. After that she had threatened that she was going to tell me that Maude was incontinent if the will was not changed to include her.

It all sounded incredulous, a plot out of a mystery novel with the murdered person being this poor little lady named Maude.

Bu then the story got even more complicated and scary. Terry also threatened Maude with going to a nursing home, since she could not live in the house independently any longer. Terry threatened that she was going to notify the health authorities and they were going to force Maude to move into a nursing home.

I could not leave Maude in the house with Terry and her boyfriend. Diane and I packed her and Puddings into my car, and I took them home with me.

The picture had now changed. Maude needed to have a person living with her, and Terry and her friend had to move out of Maude's house. As we were leaving, I went downstairs and looked for some telephone books or whatever Maude had with names of people that I could contact. Diane helped me sift through the book and we found Yvonne's number circled repeatedly with many Maude doodles around it.

I drove Maude to my house and settled her in our guest room. I used a big garbage bag under the mattress pad and locked my cat Donny away from Puddings.

The situation was too complicated, and I was losing control. Hugh suggested I call Yvonne. He was concerned that Yvonne could accuse me of meddling in Maude's affairs and finances.

The next day I served Maude breakfast and I gave Puddings some scrambled eggs. I tried to help her to the bathroom. We did not have any accidents. It was a nice summer weekend, and I took Maude and Puddings down by our pool and garden. Maude seemed to be happy, but after a while she started to get this vague look as she looked across the blue pool. That same stare as before when we were talking about the '20s.

I asked her if I could get her something to drink, but she said that she wanted to go back home.

"I want to go home. I do not trust that we locked it up correctly and don't know what that Terry is going to be up to at my house."

I told Maude that I needed to call Yvonne for help to straighten out the situation because I did not know what to do with Terry, and Yvonne was older and more experienced than me.

I never made a mention of wills and other such things that were none of my business. Maude, to my and Hugh's relief, agreed that we should call Yvonne. The telephone call was made and Yvonne agreed to come in a couple of days.

* * *

Before I took Maude home, I thought it wise to swing by the University Health Service. We went to urgent care. We left Puddings in the car. She was barking wildly and I thought she might have a heart attack. I dragged Maude into the ER and I requested a wheelchair. I was worried about Maude's need for the bathroom. As it was early in the morning, we did not have to wait for too long.

We were taken to a room and waited for the doctor. The nurse checked Maude's blood pressure and wanted to know what brought us to the ER. I told her that I wanted to have Maude checked out because she was not feeling too good and I had just come back from being out of town for a month. The nurse wanted to know where Maude lived and who was taking care of her. I told her that she owned a rooming house in Dinkytown and there were many girls who were looking after her. I told her that currently some girls were moving in and some out. The nurse wanted to know what my relationship to her was.

Maude interrupted her and said, "Helen is my best friend and helper."

The nurse ran out and came back with the doctor. There was more examining and more questions.

"Does she live with you, and do you have power of attorney for her?" the doctor asked.

"No, but the person who does is coming into town today."

"She cannot live alone. I don't think that she is capable…"

"Yes, the person with the power of attorney will take care of all of this. I'm just helping till she arrives."

"She cannot live in the rooming house by herself. Is that understood?"

"Totally," I said.

I was thinking that I had made a mistake by bringing her to the doctor's office. I was beginning to hate this young jerk…

"She is a candidate for a nursing home," he blurted.

"What are you talking about? She's with me and we're going to go to her house, and I'll put her in bed, and her other friend with the power of attorney will meet us there soon!"

I looked at Maude—her cheeks were all flushed and her eyes were about to tear up.

"I just wanted you to check her blood pressure. We don't need any of your advice on how to live."

"Yes, but you are responsible if anything happens to her…" he said with a huff.

"Come on, Maude. Let's get out of here," I said. We got up and slowly walked out of the room and to my car.

Maude felt very relieved to be out of that situation.

"I'm sorry I took you there," I said.

"I don't think they ever have anything to offer except mean words," she said.

"My father used to say that a good doctor should always put himself in his patient's shoes and walk three meters. That guy had never done such a thing. He was a dum-dum," I replied.

I wanted to use worse words to describe him but did not want to shock poor Maude. We drove to her house, and I settled her in and then drove home and waited for Yvonne to show up.

* * *

My involvement with Maude was purely a "friends' love affair." People who knew Maude and me could not understand what that meant. My Hellenic culture and the family that I came from cultivated in me a sense of obligation to other humans even if there was no reward in it for me. My father had devoted his life to medicine, never asking for more money or denying anyone services. My mother made social services her life's work. My grandfather told me how he once helped an old classmate end his alcoholism. The classmate's family kept asking what they could do for my grandfather. But he told them he did not need anything, and so did not want anything in return. Going all the way back to my grandparents, there was a firm belief that we were here in this world to be of help to other humans.

Chapter 6

When she arrived, Yvonne straightened out the house and hired a woman to take care of Maude. Terry and the boyfriend became history.

I was pleased that Maude would stay in her house and that a person was going to be looking after her. She moved Maude into the little room that was Maude's mother's room and the woman, whose name was Florence, moved into Margaret's old room.

I talked to Maude every day and visited her often. Florence would call me and let me know how things were going in the house. They still had a couple of girls staying there, but they were very selective.

Florence would also tell me about Yvonne's efforts to obtain power of attorney which meant complete control over Maude's finances. She told me that Maude wanted to be in charge though. She did not want someone else, even Yvonne, to take over. Florence wanted me to explain to Maude that she had to give Yvonne power of attorney. So, I did, even though I felt that it was not a kind thing to do, but Maude's estate affairs were totally out of my hands. She had created this situation by making this will and not even bothering to tell me about it. Perhaps that was a petty feeling, and I should have been ashamed of it but so be it. I was glad all the horrible tenants had moved out of Maude's life. Yvonne was doing good things, but she was also a major beneficiary of all of Maude's assets. She did it in a very sly way and I never understood how she outsmarted Maude. I felt she was a professional predator and if she tried to do something that would really hurt Maude, I would go after her.

It was December 12, 1980, when Florence called me. I remember that I was home writing Christmas cards, and my son was watching *Mister Rogers*. It was a four-day week for us, and Friday was a great opportunity to get something done at home. Florence told me that Maude could not walk, and that Yvonne's attorney was going to be over to the house at any moment to have Maude sign all the papers and transfer all her money into a joint account with Yvonne. I asked if Maude was faking it, but she assured me that she did not look too good. I grabbed my boy, and we drove to Maude's. I was aware that she might have had a stroke, as her father did. I did not want to scare her by calling an ambulance.

Florence and I carried her into my car. She had gotten that vague look on her face again, like she was seeing some long-lost relatives. Quickly though, she focused her eyes on my little boy. She was observing every one of his movements. I can still hear her saying, "He is just so great. I bet you could not have made him any more perfect even if you tried."

Puddings yelped and barked, and I thought that she was going to die right on the spot.

"Take care of my Puddings. Take care of my puppy," Maude said repeatedly all the way to the University Hospital.

I later tried to find meaning in what Maude was saying during that scene. I felt that she knew that she was never going to see Puddings and my son again.

Maude was admitted to the hospital with a mild stroke. The doctor told her so and I repeated it to her.

"Oh, that's not a nice thing to say," she told me.

I knew she was afraid of strokes, and I felt guilty for telling her. I will never forgive myself for opening my big mouth.

"I hope she'll be able to go home in a few days," I said.

"You can hope," the doctor said.

I hoped he wouldn't say anything more in front of her and grabbed him by the sleeve and dragged him towards the open door. He was kind of shocked by my gesture, but now he was out of Maude's hearing range.

"She is a strong woman, and she has made it through many hard times," I said.

"She is ancient," he smirked.

"So? What does that make her? Non-existent?"

"You hippies all have big hearts, but you're putting stress on the medical system—and please don't grab me again," he said in one breath.

"I had to get you away from her before you gave her another stroke. I apologize for touching you, but you were forgetting your bedside manner," I said and I walked back into the room where Maude was.

I did not turn around to see his reaction. I gave Maude a hug and told her I would be back the next day and we would take her home.

* * *

I drove Florence back to 1018 and then I needed to take my boy home. We drove quietly back to our house. I kept turning the radio on and off when my ear caught the following: "Arm & Hammer paid five million for Da Vinci's notebook."

"Wow," I thought, "I wonder what Maude's scribbled notes could sell for. She is not Da Vinci, of course, but she is an important person—at least she was once. She is an important person to us who will always love her. She's been resilient and fiercely independent her whole life."

I wondered how old Da Vinci was when he created that notebook. There were other people who worked into late age. Goya created the *Black Paintings* in his eighties and claimed that he was still learning. Renoir painted while he was suffering from arthritis. They all had the same kind of resilience and courage to keep hanging in there and just to keep trying to live the best way they could.

When I got home, I called Yvonne to tell her what had happened, and Florence took Puddings home to her mother.

Maude was never to return to 1018 4th St. S.E. While she was at the hospital, she had multiple strokes and lost her vision. I bought her a Christmas tree with little glass ornaments and put it on her dressing table hoping that when her vision returned, she would wake up and see it. I knew, though, that she would not get any better and I prayed for her to die peacefully. Maude would rather be dead than an invalid in a nursing home.

And one cold January morning she did die.

It was strange because I had been thinking of her for a couple of days and decided to go to the hospital to see her. She was in a room by herself. Her mouth was open and her eyes were shut as if she was in a deep sleep. Her curly hair was straight and white now. She wore a blue and white hospital gown, and she was partly covered with a sheet. The oxygen tubes were lying on her pillow. I went out of the room to look for a nurse. We both walked back into the room together. The nurse touched my arm and said, "She died just now. I'm sorry."

The struggle was over. I rubbed her foot, and a reflex went through her body.

"Goodbye, my friend," I said. "I love you. Goodbye, Maude."

* * *

The next day I met Yvonne at Maude's house to plan the funeral. We found a clipping of a notice for the memorial service for Maude's mother, and I suggested doing everything the same. We went to the funeral home that Maude had used for her mother. Yvonne tried to get the cheapest casket and services. I insisted that she had to do everything as Maude did for her mother. She did not want to fight me, and I was beginning to turn into a "witch," taking after my friend. I found myself arguing with Yvonne as to who did the most for Maude. And she accused me of wanting to take Maude's Tiffany lamp.

I was disgusted at myself and my pettiness, but most of all I was sick of Yvonne.

The funeral director asked us what kind of music we wanted to play. I thought for a while and then I said, "Play 'Eleanor Rigby.'"

"The Beatles!" exclaimed Yvonne. "Well, at least I'm glad you're not asking them to play 'Here Comes the Bride.'"

I felt like Yvonne and I were light-years apart, though we had the same friend in common, Maude.

I felt that in the end the director was more on my side because it was a complete Beatles service. He found all my favorite songs and on that gloomy January morning, they were a ray of sunshine. She was buried in the family plot next to her mother.

There were very few of her friends there and after the funeral we all dispersed and never saw each other again.

As I was leaving the cemetery *The Great Gatsby* came to my mind again: "So we beat on, boats against the current, borne back ceaselessly into the past."

* * *

Some of the things that Maude gave me are scattered throughout all my houses. When I see them, I remember her and think that things live longer than people. They may be separated from their owner, but they still have their owner's soul.

* * *

Now I am old, and deal with some of Maude's issues and loneliness, and when something exciting happens to me and I want to share it with someone, I experience a déjà vu moment and turn my head to tell it to her…

Maude lived a courageous life. I remember my grandfather telling me about a poem by poet Nazim Hikmet:

Life is not a joke,
You will take it
Seriously, yes seriously, like a squirrel does
Without waiting for anything from outside or
from far away
You have nothing else to do but live.

And that's what Maude did.

Epilogue

Adam Bradshaw Hauge
489-1349

Hart

Maude C., of 1018 4th St. SE. Survived by friends, nieces, nephews & cousins. "I beg of you, do not forget me, when the phenomenon of death visits me. Oh, keep my memory alive, for if you forget me, only then will I have surely died." Services Tues. 10 am at the Washburn McReavy-Southeast Chapel, 2nd St. & Central Ave. SE. Interment Sunset Memorial Park. Friends may call 1 hour before time of service.

Heltemes

Gerald J., age 57, of 3135 Rhode Island So. Employee of Superior Plating. Survived by

> Hart, Maude C. of 1018 4th St. SE. Survived by friends, nieces, nephews, cousins. "I beg you do not forget me, when the phenomenon of death visits me. Oh, keep my memory alive, for if you forget me, only then will I have surely died."
>
> Services, Tuesday 10 am at the Washburn McReavy-Southeast Chapel, 2nd St & Central Ave SE.
>
> Internment [at] Sunset, Memorial Park. Friends may call 1 hour before time of service.

That was her obituary. She was just a few weeks short of her ninetieth birthday. Her life was well lived, under often unusual circumstances and during very rapidly changing times.

I don't remember how the obituary was written and by whom. Perhaps the funeral director concocted it after talking with me; I am following her directive and trying to write down something about her in hopes that she will not be forgotten, though almost forty-five years have gone by.

Three or four years ago, I was driving down 4th Street SE and was shocked to see that Maude's house was gone and an ugly house had been built in its place. It lacked the elegance and grace of Maude's house. It was squeezed in the lot and thrown together with modern materials, asymmetric shapes, and utilitarian spaces, a failure of modern architecture, adding to the anonymity of all the newly constructed buildings that are now everywhere in our beloved Dinkytown, which has lost all its charm.

Site of Maude's old house

Very few sorority and fraternity houses remain and there is no preservation of any of the unique and quaint buildings. I looked through my old photos and finally found a picture of Maude's house.

She hoped that her house could have survived her. She was always very generous about giving people some of her things; she just did not want people to steal them. I remember when my brother had moved to Minneapolis, she asked me if he had any furniture and finding out that he did not, she invited him to come and take some of the furniture she was not using.

I was impressed with her gesture. I said, "Maude, it was very nice of you to do that."

"Oh well, he will remember me when he looks at it after I'm gone," she murmured.

I was kind of saddened by those words, but she was a realist. Maude had hoped that she could leave something behind. Isn't this what all of us human beings hope for? So she still lives on with us—in memory, in things, in words—forever.

Acknowledgements

Thanks to the staff at Calumet Editions for taking on my little project. I also want to thank my editor Emily Trenholm, and all the Calumet staff for putting up with my shortcomings with Microsoft Word. Then, thanks go to my son Alexandros Lindsay who encouraged me to resurrect a story I wrote thirty-five years ago. Special gratitude to my son Theodore Lindsay who took the time out of his busy life to edit all my images and give life to the story. I must acknowledge the Hennepin County Library for preserving the old images of our beloved Dinkytown and making them available. Finally, special thanks are owed to the little old lady from 4th St. SE, Maude Hart, who was my inspiration and my best friend for life.

About the Author

Helen Electrie Lindsay was born in Thessaloniki, Greece. She graduated from Anatolia College in Thessaloniki and came to the United States on a Fulbright scholarship to study physics. She worked for Dayton Hudson, and as an engineering product manager at MTS Systems in the Twin Cities. She is the author of *Written on the Knee: A Diary from the Greek-Italian Front of WWII*, and lives in Wayzata, Minnesota

www.ingramcontent.com/pod-product-compliance
Lightning Source LLC
LaVergne TN
LVHW051013080826
845145LV00009B/2591

* 9 7 8 1 9 6 2 8 3 4 7 3 5 *